An
Occasional
Thought

M. Loretta Daly

PublishAmerica
Baltimore

First printing

ISBN: 1-4137-5799-5
PUBLISHED BY PUBLISHAMERICA, LLLP
www.publishamerica.com
Baltimore

Printed in the United States of America

Dedicated to my husband,
John

To my children,
Brian, Cindy, Tim and Ken

And to my grandchildren,
Ryan, Brittany, Jenna, Heather and Ben

Dandelions

Who was the one who made the rules
That we must now obey?
Who took a joy of childhood
And tossed it far away?

The once loved dandelion
Its sunny face aglow
Has joined the now forbidden
Where childish dreams must go

The sweat pours from our brows
We must eradicate
The treasure of our youthful years
The flower we've come to hate

Day to day and year to year
Our vigil we must keep
For if we turn away just once
Into our lawn it creeps

The flowers we have chosen
The ones we choose to sow
Take time and work and money
And sometimes just won't grow

Lilacs, roses, daisies
Are in our hearts to stay
But the smiling dandelion
Centers every child's bouquet

With the spirit of the lion
Its sturdy stalks grow tall
Its seeds are sown by children
A lesson to us all

Boredom

Boredom comes when life is good
When trauma's not in view
Every day remains the same
No bad has come to you

We never should resent it
The time will surely come
When we'll long to return
To what we called "humdrum"

Sameness is a gift
On which we can rely
It lends a sense of safety
To a distant troubled sky

Possessions

I never owned a thing
That I could do without
I never walk into a store
And not bring something out

It's a losing situation
That I will never win
The only basket on my desk
Is one that's labeled "IN"

The day has finally come
With house filled to the brim
The door no longer opens
And I'm outside looking in

Autumn –
The Forgotten Child

Spring is nature's lovely child
With blessings from above
Summer has her golden days
To assure her of our love

Winter has a snow-white coat
And holidays galore
But Autumn is the forgotten child
But it is so much more

Autumn is my favorite
I'll try to tell you why
The beauty of the painted leaves
Against a sunless sky

Autumn is an open door
To good times just ahead
The crispness of the moonlit night
The smell of fresh-baked bread

The childish joy of Halloween
The jack-o'-lantern's grin
The candy apple's crunch so sweet
The cider on your chin

First days of school bring memories
Of years when we were young
The fear of the new teacher
The friendships just begun

All are born and also die
They do it all year long
Autumn brings it home to us
In fact – in verse – in song

She whispers to us who we are
And who we soon will be
And those we loved – who now are gone
Also speak to me

She brings us to remember
The times that went before
Like all the leaves of Summer
That now carpet Autumn's floor

Autumn feeds the winter
She provides for everything
She takes us through the coldest days
And safely into Spring

Talking To Yourself

When talking to yourself
Nothing's a surprise
There are no revelations
No opening of the eyes

You've heard it all before
And surely will again
But somehow you're not bored
You're talking to a friend

Faces

The faces we present
Are myriad at least
One will see the lamb
The next will see the beast

It is a human trait
Not one to make us proud
We save our worst for those we love
Our smiles are for the crowd

The outside world will soon be gone
Its love is never true
When you turn for home again
Who'll be there for you?

Tomorrow's Mirror

The truth is told within the eyes
Beware the tongue with brazen lies
Unsettled is the paper crown
It soon lies shredded on the ground

Fleeting fortunes falsely gleam
They never will be what they seem
Tomorrow's mirror must reflect
The sins of those who did defect

Honor borne and honor born
Will sanctify the misty morn
Of those whose hearts are good and just
The ones who earn our faith and trust

The race not won by swift of feet
But patient plodding down the street
Is sweeter still than stolen gold
Purloined by heart of arctic mold

Exchanges

We can't achieve wisdom
Without adding years
We cannot gain knowledge
Without shedding tears

We cannot mature
And not have to pay
For all that we add
We give some away

Exchanges are made
Every day that we live
The decision is ours
What to take, what to give

Storm Warnings

Off to the grocery
I must prepare
For the snow they say
Will fly everywhere

The parking lot's crowded
As far as you see
To find a close spot
Is not meant to be

We all bundle in
And manage to smile
Through each traffic jam
In each narrow aisle

My cart slowly fills
And there straight ahead
I spy on the shelf
The last loaf of bread

In a moment of doubt
I now hesitate
To grab the last loaf
Would be in bad taste

I need not have worried
From back in the line
A tall, burly man
Grabbed the loaf that was mine!

With pioneer spirit
I now am empowered
With packets of yeast
And a large bag of flour

I wait in a line
Of impossible length
I will stand the test
If I just have the strength

The carry-out boy
Waves as I drive away
"Thanks very much
And have a nice day!"

Today Belongs to Me

I'm waiting for tomorrow
Then all will be fine
This is a foolish game
Today is all that's mine

If I wait till later
What's now is no more
The chance that was today
Will be a bolted door

Tomorrow will come never
Today belongs to me
When I live with what I have
Then I will be free

Maturity

Some achieve it early
Some just never do
An unselfish love for others
Will bring it home to you

To take the pain of others
And claim it as your own
To try to ease their suffering
Is maturity full-blown

When you feel their pain
Deep within your soul
With no thought of yourself
You've reached life's purest goal

Memories of You

Everything you say
And everything you do
Remain when you are gone
These are memories of you

Once the word is said
Once the deed is done
It does not belong to you
It belongs to everyone

TV Or Not TV

There is a plain square box
That sits within the room
It looks so innocent
But has become my tomb

When I sit before it
My life ceases to be
I live in it through others
In a world they made for me

My imagination
Is a thing out of the past
With no life of my own
I'm now one of the cast

While I am living their life
Who is living mine?
It all becomes confused
This exchange of space and time

Will I no longer know
What is real and what is not?
I must somehow awake
To the life that I forgot

I am sorry that I wasted
What belongs to me
I will learn from my mistakes
Say… What is on TV???

Was It Important?

Was it important?
What you had to say?
Yesterday you said it
But I thought of it today

I nodded as you spoke
And I made a vague reply
But what you said escapes me
And now I wonder why

You are so special to me
And I always will regret
That words you chose to speak to me
I let myself forget

I took you so for granted
And now I take a vow
If you will give me one more chance
I'll listen to you now

Just Tell Monday, "No"

The weekend should be longer
I have places yet to go
It is always inconvenient
Can I just tell Monday, "No"?

There are shops I have not shopped in
Broadway has a brand new show
The fishing hole is calling
Can I just tell Monday, "No"?

I have not finished sleeping
The grass I did not mow
I need a few more hours
Can I just tell Monday, "No"?

Next week will be different
There will be no tale of woe
Next week it's a promise
That I won't tell Monday, "No"

The Town of "Never Me"

"Not Guilty" was the verdict
No wrong could they see
Something is amiss
In the town of "Never Me"

No one to take the blame
No one is wrong you see
Justice is stone blind
In the town of "Never Me"

Ignorance is ugly
To a soul that would be free
Truth has been forsaken
In the town of "Never Me"

Self

I think they all are judging
But when I look to see
I find that those I feared the most
Took little note of me

Thinking just of self
Is a journey to alone
Inward thoughts do little good
To right a world gone wrong

A Knock Upon My Door

The whole world was before me once
My course was set back then
The time would come – I'd win it all
I can't remember when

There was so much to learn
I could not learn it all
I hope the things that passed me by
Never come to call

If there's a knock upon my door
And a voice that I don't know
I'll pretend that I'm not home
And let my chances go

Final Stop

I'd like to be the final stop
Not the "on the way"
Detours are not popular
Not where you'd choose to stay

Our lives are always changing
Though we sometimes do not know
The simple state of being
Will prove that this is so

He Will Never Know You, Dad

When he looks into my eyes
His eyes a blaze of blue
I feel a lump within my throat
That blue belonged to you

His life he'll live without you
It is so very sad
You had so much to teach him, but
He will never know you, Dad

His life began when yours was done
He'll never know your smile
It would have meant so much
If he had known you for a while

Tired of Being Brave

I want to run, I want to play
I want to skip and shout
I want to do all the things
That childhood is about

I am only nine years old
My life has just begun
Yet, I have missed so many things
That make a young life fun

I get so tired of being brave
I want to wail and cry
I want to know just why
The good times pass me by

I really don't deserve this
What fate has done to me
Please try to understand
I just want to be free

Please don't think I'm naughty
Please don't think I'm bad
I only want for just a while
What others always had

It probably won't happen
This dream I keep inside
So the things I whisper to you, God
From others I must hide

Someday when I am with you
Please take me on your knee
And tell me, God, of all the kids
Why did you choose me?

Who Will Be My Daddy?

I hear Daddy yell at Mommy
And she yells back at him
I sit here in the shadows
With my little brother, Jim

We hold on to each other
We are all that we have got
Why are they so angry?
Is it my fault? Is it not?

If they really loved us
Would they make us feel this way?
As we cry away the hours
And wish night into day

I don't want to lose my daddy
It just really isn't fair
Who will be my daddy
When my daddy isn't there?

They said we were a family
But it really isn't so
My family had a daddy
Will I be the next to go?

Take Care

Take care what you speak
Heed what you say
A word you may add
But not take away

An Easy Thing to Say

"I love you" comes so easily
It's an easy thing to say
Living love is harder
It's a test from day to day

Is it real or is it not?
How are you to know?
It's really very simple
Love will always grow

Love will stand the trials of time
Love will see us through
The problems life has thrown our way
Were faced by me and you

We bolstered one another
We faced the world as one
We still will be together
When our last day here is done

Reality

Sometimes my body
Is a little less than kind
You're four score it reminds me
Though I'm two score in my mind

It sometimes is so pleasant
Remembering who I was
My brain likes to pretend
Though my body never does

It's time to sit down now
Reality must win
Old age is not easy
For the youthful you within

The Early Bus

Oatmeal, juice & buttered toast
To calm the morning fuss
Sentinel bookbags by the door
Await the early bus

Did you remember? Don't forget
Departing calls ring out
Be careful nows & I love yous
The timeless mother's shout

The silence now is all too loud
The bus melts from our view
We think of all the little things
That we forgot to do

Did we take time to give a hug
To the child who spilled his drink?
Or were we too impatient?
Too organized to think?

The time now is unlimited
To analyze our deeds
In everything we do and say
We plant the future's seeds

We vow we will do better
The remainder of the day
The next morn will be perfect
As we send them on their way

Just a Dog

They know not from where they came
They don't know that they'll die
They never ask you why they live
They never wonder why

Their trust in you is total
Their love beyond compare
The greatest wish they ever have
Is time you let them share

The imperfections that we have
They will never see
You are their God upon this earth
Until they cease to be

The death of one so faithful
Is a loss so hard to bear
We always will remember
The time when they were there

Love Arrived

Love arrived at eight o'clock
I slept in till nine
Now too late I realize
It is gone and it was mine

Regrets will be forever
Some things just don't wait
My heart resides with sleepy eyes
Outside Love's garden gate

The Death of Yesterday

I mourn the death of yesterday
Yet celebrate today
One must die so one may live
There is no other way

Days I miss that are no more
Will ever haunt my mind
The life I loved and lived before
Was born of ties that bind

How do we finally accept
That what was is no more?
Today's prints are now in the sand
Beside the ocean door

Only One

The young man lived within your eyes
A story to be told
How sad that we must realize
The young die with the old

The young man full of promise
His song waits to be sung
Future generations gone
The old die with the young

Popularity

It's easy to be popular
If you never take a stand
If you never rock a single boat
You're always in demand

No one listens anyway
If they don't agree
I guess we should drift aimlessly
Upon a mindless sea

Strengthen or Destroy

Tell him that he's handsome
Tell her that she's fair
The rest of their lives
Will be with those who do not care

Of course they are not perfect
They won't always be the best
This they should not hear from you
They will hear it from the rest

Those warm trusting souls
Should never know a fear
Surround them with your love
Let them know you will be near

Their egos are so fragile
Their confidence is young
To strengthen or destroy
Is in the power of a tongue

The Bridge from You to Me

I have tried so hard to cross it
But it's very hard to see
The crossing is not easy
The bridge from you to me

I'm not really certain
How it came to be
But its existence is important
The bridge from you to me

If it ever crumbled
My soul would ne'er be free
It is my very lifeline
The bridge from you to me

Dust to Dust

It once was so important
The dust atop the shelf
Its presence was a huge disgrace
I blamed it on myself

Day by day I chased it
I could not let it stay
What would people think
If I let it have its way?

The years slipped by, as on I fought
The game was never won
The dust just seemed to mock me
My work was never done

I no longer chase the dust
I gave up finally
I'm just too tired to fight it
As it settles over me

Twenty Years

Twenty years in which to grow
Then twenty years in which to know
That we were at our very best
From the time we left the nest

Twenty more and we will find
That others cease to be as kind
As in the twenty gone before
Which are gone forevermore

Add to these another score
You'll likely see us nevermore
Our time is brief before the door
That opens on a distant shore

How Not Alone I Was

I think back to another time
As every widow does
The people – people – people
How not alone I was

The children and the laughter
Our world was one called love
The hustle and the bustle
How not alone I was

The holidays were so much fun
The house was all abuzz
We had not one dull moment
How not alone I was

Your world can change so quickly
Like lightning from above
I now live with the memories
How not alone I was

Habits

Habits are expressions
Of an us we cannot hide
Some things are beyond control
And cannot be denied

At times we must regress
To what brought us to be
Habits are an unseen urge
The need to just be me

An Occasional Thought

The diapers she changed
The toys that she bought
Where is she now?
An occasional thought

The cookies she baked
The manners she taught
Where is she now?
An occasional thought

She nursed you through
Every illness you caught
Where is she now?
An occasional thought

When hurt or afraid
It was her that you sought
Where is she now?
An occasional thought

The love that she gave
The smiles that she brought
Where is she now?
An occasional thought

She lived just for you
Your battles she fought
Where is she now?
An occasional thought

A Place Called Me and You

It's the little things that hurt
That cause the deepest pain
It's the turning of a corner
That can ne'er be turned again

Nothing can replace
The joys that I have known
The eager, happy faces
That greeted me at dawn

It's the upturned youthful face
That slowly fades from view
It's the ending of an era
A place called me and you

A Mother's Prayer

We who wash the dishes
We who scrub the floors
We who do the ironing
And other thankless chores

Our efforts go unnoticed
Our faces are a blur
Our time on Earth is tethered
To the household's daily whir

At times it seems so futile
At times it seems insane
The frenzy never ending
Our efforts seem in vain

Time has a way of calling us
The treadmill finally slows
And suddenly we realize
This is the life we chose

We will miss the dishes
We will miss the chores
We will miss the hand prints
And the mud upon the floors

Our life at last we realize
Was full beyond compare
The emptiness surrounds us
As we pray this mother's prayer

Forgive us, God, for our complaints
When our life was so good
We didn't know it way back then
We never understood

We miss those little faces
We miss the trusting eyes
We wish we had just one more chance
The backward glance is wise

Be Kind

You might not even notice them
When walking down the street
Each bears a marked resemblance
To others that you meet

However, each is special
Each one is unique
One look into those soulful eyes
Brings truth to what I speak

Each one is a daughter or
Each one is a son
Each brought the joy of Heaven
When life had just begun

Please be kind to all you meet
Please greet them with a smile
Remember, God gave each a chance
To be here for a while

The Eternal Pup

Puppies are sweet
They are lots of fun
They bring to your home
Little lives just begun

For all they need
They depend on you
It remains the same
Their whole lives through

Puppies are children
Who never grow up
He will need you always
This eternal pup

He will get into mischief
He will make a mess
He will cause you all kinds
Of emotional stress

Don't give up on him
Ask help from above
He trusts you with his life
And thanks you with his love

One Slip

Would you like to be revered?
Well, frankly, so would I
But that requires perfection
Or a willingness to die

You could be a scoundrel
You could cheat and lie
But when you're six feet under
There's a tear in every eye

Perfection's not so easy
It must be your whole life long
One slip is all it takes
To turn right into wrong

Monsters in the Shadows

I am all alone now
And I am so afraid
Monsters in the shadows
Where earlier I played

"Honey, don't be silly,"
My mommy said to me
"You know there are no monsters,"
And she closed the door firmly

If I am very quiet
And close my eyes real tight
The monsters might not see me
And I'll make it through the night

Naptime

A blankie, a pillow
A ragged old bear
The cherubic face
The dark, tousled hair

The long curled lashes
The cute baby nose
A sweet little angel
In peaceful repose

Just Another Day

In a time so long ago
In a place so far away
This date was once so special
Now it's just another day

All eyes were on us then
As we stood side by side
We vowed to love each other
I would always be your bride

The years stretched out before us
And we always understood
We would face the world together
Both the bad times and the good

The good times – there were many
The bad times showed up, too
But I knew that we would make it
With the Us made strong by you

Those times live on in memory
Alone now I must stay
Tomorrow should be special
But it's just another day

Life's Unkindest Blow

Love creates the deepest pain
That we will ever know
The more we care, the more we hurt
It's life's unkindest blow

The closer that it comes
The more natural it seems
Faces that were in my life
Now echo in my dreams

Minutes

The minutes that we waste
We choose to give away
They cannot be reclaimed
They're of another day

Let's hope that we have learned
From mistakes that we have made
We must not multiply
The price that has been paid

No One Is Immune

Why am I so haunted
By the pain-filled eyes I see?
Reflected in their tears
Is a future also me

No one is immune
To what lies just ahead
We all must face tomorrow
With a certain sense of dread

In every life there comes a day
To pay for times enjoyed
A time in each and every life
We wish we could avoid

Acceptance is so difficult
It means that we have lost
A time so precious to us
A bridge that must be crossed

The Suddenly Alone

I am so very thankful
For the joys that I have known
But pain is so much deeper
To the suddenly alone

The quiet filters through the noise
It just won't go away
The more I try to cover it
The more it seems to stay

I know that it is selfish
To think of only me
But when your heart is broken
Me is all that you can see

A Means of Survival

It's a means of survival
This easing of the pain
If not allowed to happen
The rest would be in vain

I view as from a distance
What is much too close
Life has a way of healing
With a daily living dose

I don't look for you anymore
I will not see you there
But your warmth is always in my heart
Your shadow's everywhere

You Taught Me How to Love

Each unencumbered thought
Each happy point of view
Is escorted by guilt
Since the day that I lost you

How dare I survive?
It just isn't somehow fair
For a day to bring a smile
That you're not here to share

This grief is never gone
I can't bear any more
Everywhere I turn
I find a bolted door

You are a part of me
I'll never let you leave
You taught me how to love
Now you've taught me how to grieve

Would You Really Want to Know?

We wonder where we're going
We wonder how we'll go
But if you had the option
Would you really want to know?

The wonder of the moment
The thrill of what's to be
Would tarnish with the knowledge
Of the future you and me

The Absence of You

When you long for what was
You deny what must be
They are born of two times
One was us – one is me

It is hard to give up
The world we once knew
And open my eyes
To the absence of you

The Month of My Despair

May is the month of my despair
I'll face it every year
My heart will break with memories
Of the time when he was here

As we go on, the good and bad
Will be assigned their times
Our life's too short to agonize
Finding reasons – finding rhymes

Honor them with memories
Not extended grief
Sorrow born in yesterday
Must somehow find relief

Good things happen every day
Bad things happen, too
The ones allowed to rule your days
Are really up to you

Shed your tears in private
Then turn a brighter face
And give your smiles to those who wait
Today's their rightful place

Printed in the United States
24798LVS00001B/226-231